THE
HORROR MOVIE NIGHT
COOKBOOK

60 DELICIOUSLY DEADLY RECIPES INSPIRED BY ICONIC SLASHERS, ZOMBIE FILMS, PSYCHOLOGICAL THRILLERS, SCI-FI SPOOKS, & MORE

RICHARD S. SARGENT

ULYSSES PRESS

Published by:
ULYSSES PRESS
PO Box 3440
Berkeley, CA 94703
www.ulyssespress.com

ISBN: 978-1-64604-491-7
Library of Congress Control Number: 2023930762

Printed in China
10 9 8 7 6 5 4 3 2 1

Acquisitions editor: Kierra Sondereker
Managing editor: Claire Chun
Editor: Susan Lang
Proofreader: Renee Rutledge
Front cover design: Raquel Castro
Interior design: Winnie Liu
Recipe photos: © Nevyana Dimitrova
Artwork: front cover and section icons © Tobiha_neru/shutterstock.com; drinking game glass
    © eduardonunez/shutterstock.com
Production: Jake Flaherty Design

For Josh, my slicing and dicing partner.

CONTENTS

INTRODUCTION

History of the Horror Movie Night

My friends told me that they knew very little about the horror genre, and honestly I can't say I was shocked. When people think of the horror genre, they think of bad acting, gratuitous nudity, and senseless violence. Sure, there's some of that. However, a lot of horror films use the genre to make a statement. A great horror film holds a mirror up to society in the hopes that it will make us think and change for the better. As a student of horror (I know, gag), I felt it was my duty to introduce my friends to what are generally considered to be some of the essential and important genre films.

I couldn't just pop a movie into the DVD player and order a pizza, though. Where's the creativity in that? I started hosting Horror Movie Nights, where we would sink our teeth into an evening of three films, all connected by a common theme. Each carefully selected film would inspire a different meal course and cocktail pairing. The recipes that follow are based on some of my personal favorite films,

some of the classics, and some scary flicks that are just fun.

On the next page I'll show you how I broke down my movie nights, but I encourage you to alter the recipes as you see fit. Just be creative with the portion sizes.

If you purchased this book for yourself or received it as a gift, you must be a horror nut like me, so thank you! My friends and I had a hell of a time testing and perfecting these recipes, and I hope you have a killer time when you take a stab at re-creating them for your own movie nights.

I should mention that you will not find kitschy Pinterest recipes—like brownies shaped like ghosts with googly eyes—in this book. These are actual recipes inspired by the content of the films, not Halloween decorations.

Now, in the infamous words of Julie James...

What are you waiting for?

How I Organize My Own Horror Movie Nights

HORROR MOVIE NIGHT THEMES

1. My Personal Favorites

APPETIZER: *Scream* (1996)

MAIN COURSE: *The Descent* (2005)

DESSERT: *Event Horizon* (1997)

2. From Woodsboro to the Woods

APPETIZER: *The Blair Witch Project* (1999)

MAIN COURSE: *Scream 2* (1997)

DESSERT: *The Evil Dead* (1981)

3. Supernatural

APPETIZER: *Poltergeist* (1982)

MAIN COURSE: *Stir of Echoes* (1999)

DESSERT: *The Conjuring* (2013)

4. Summer Slashing

APPETIZER: *I Know What You Did Last Summer* (1997)

MAIN COURSE: *Broken Lizard's Club Dread* (2004)

DESSERT: *Jaws* (1975)

5. Horror Hotels

APPETIZER: *Identity* (2003)

MAIN COURSE: *Psycho* (1960)

DESSERT: *Bug* (2006)

6. Zombie Night

APPETIZER: *Dawn of the Dead* (2004)

MAIN COURSE: *Shaun of the Dead* (2004)

DESSERT: *Night of the Living Dead* (1968)

7. When Animals Attack

APPETIZER: *Crawl* (2019)

MAIN COURSE: *Cujo* (1983)

DESSERT: *The Birds* (1963)

8. Holiday Horror

APPETIZER: *The Wicker Man* (1973)

MAIN COURSE: *Halloween* (1978)

DESSERT: *Black Christmas* (1974)

9. Deadly Disease

APPETIZER: *28 Days Later* (2002)

MAIN COURSE: *Contagion* (2011)

DESSERT: *Cabin Fever* (2002)

10. Summer Slashing, the Shriekquel

APPETIZER: *Piranha* (1978)

MAIN COURSE: *The Ruins* (2008)

DESSERT: *Tucker and Dale vs. Evil* (2010)

FINGER FOODS

SCREAM (1996)

In what is arguably one of the best openings to any horror film ever, Casey Becker is seen making Jiffy Pop while she chats it up with Ghostface on the phone. Eventually she burns the popcorn. Try not to do that.

"WHAT'S YOUR FAVORITE SCARY MOVIE" POPCORN
Movie Theater Popcorn Two Ways—Brown Butter Lemon and Garlic Parmesan

FOR THE BROWN BUTTER LEMON POPCORN:

1 bag microwave popcorn
½ cup unsalted butter
2 lemons
1 tablespoon lemon zest, for garnish

FOR THE GARLIC PARMESAN POPCORN:

1 bag microwave popcorn
3 tablespoons unsalted butter
2 cloves garlic, minced
2 tablespoons garlic salt
½ cup grated parmesan cheese

KILL LEVEL: Easy | BODY COUNT: 6 servings | PREP TIME: 10 minutes | COOK TIME: 10 minutes

1. Microwave the bags of popcorn according to package instructions.

2. Pour each bag of popcorn into its own large bowl.

3. For the brown butter lemon popcorn, in a medium saucepan, melt ½ cup of unsalted butter until it is light brown, about 1 to 2 minutes, stirring occasionally and watching closely to make sure it doesn't burn. Once it is light brown, remove it from the heat. Squeeze the juice from one whole lemon into the butter and stir. Pour it over the popcorn in one of the bowls and toss. Squeeze the other lemon directly onto the popcorn as you continue to toss. Garnish with the lemon zest and serve hot.

4. For the garlic parmesan popcorn, in a second saucepan, melt 3 tablespoons of unsalted butter, about 1 to 2 minutes, stirring occasionally. Once it is melted, add the minced garlic and stir for 1 minute. Then pour the garlic butter over the popcorn in the second bowl, making sure to cover it completely. Sprinkle the garlic salt and parmesan cheese over the popcorn and toss thoroughly. Serve hot.

THE BLOODY KNIFE

2½ ounces strawberry vodka
1 ounce raspberry liqueur
2 ounces pomegranate juice

KILL LEVEL: Easy | **BODY COUNT:** 1 drink | **PREP TIME:** 5 minutes

1. Mix all the ingredients together in a martini shaker filled with ice.

2. Shake until cold and serve in a chilled martini glass.

TIP: I like to make drinks ahead of time, especially when a large group is coming. You can make this cocktail in batches and chill them in the refrigerator until you're ready to drink up.

DRINKING GAME

Take a drink every time Ghostface uses his glove to wipe blood off the knife.

THE BLAIR WITCH PROJECT (1999)

In the film, Heather wakes up to find creepy piles of rocks around the tent she and her friends are sleeping in. Could that be a symbol of their impending doom?

CREEPY CAIRNS
Polenta Rounds Stacked with Goat Cheese and Caramelized Onions

6 tablespoons unsalted butter, divided

1 (18-ounce) tube polenta, sliced into 1-inch rounds

1 large yellow onion, sliced super thin

4 ounces smooth Gournay cheese, like Boursin

KILL LEVEL: Moderate | BODY COUNT: 6 servings | PREP TIME: 10 minutes | COOK TIME: 20 minutes

1. Melt 3 tablespoons of the butter in a skillet over medium heat.

2. Place the polenta rounds in the hot butter. Brown for about 5 minutes per side, longer if you like the polenta crispy.

3. While the polenta is frying, preheat the oven to the lowest temperature setting, between 170°F and 200°F.

4. Remove the rounds from the skillet and place them on a baking sheet. Put the baking sheet in the warm oven to keep them hot. Make sure the oven is on very low so you don't dry out the rounds.

5. Place the remaining 3 tablespoons of butter in the same skillet over low heat. Add the onion and cook until soft and lightly browned, 8 to 10 minutes.

6. To assemble the cairns, place the polenta rounds on a serving platter. Add an even amount of cheese to each round and top with the onion. Serve warm.

No deep woods ghost-hunting trip is complete without ghost stories around a campfire, but no story is more terrifying to adventurers than the nightmare they are already living.

THE CAMPFIRE SOUR

3 ounces bourbon
1 ounce lime juice
½ ounce pure maple syrup
1 sprig fresh rosemary, for garnish

KILL LEVEL: Medium | **BODY COUNT:** 1 drink | **PREP TIME:** 7 minutes

TIP: If you don't have a long lighter or match, you can always (carefully) use the flame on your gas stove to light the rosemary. Just don't burn yourself.

1. In a cocktail shaker, pour in the bourbon, lime juice, and maple syrup.

2. Add the fresh rosemary sprig to the shaker. Use a long match or lighter to set it on fire. Let it burn for a few seconds. Blow out the flame and cap the shaker for 1 minute so the liquid has time to infuse with the rosemary smoke.

3. After a minute, take the cap off the shaker and set the rosemary sprig aside.

4. Fill the shaker with ice, shake well, and dump the mixture into a rocks glass.

5. Garnish with the burnt sprig of rosemary and serve.

DRINKING GAME

Take a drink every time someone screams about a map. You might want to sip.

This is one of the first horror films I watched as a kid. I was freaked out by the scene where one of the paranormal researchers goes to the kitchen to get a midnight snack, including a steak from the refrigerator. He ends up getting a lot more than he was expecting.

CRAWLING STEAK

Seared Steak Slices on Sourdough Crisps with Artichoke–Jalapeño Spread

FOR THE STEAK:

1 (12-ounce) New York strip steak
2½ tablespoons olive oil, divided
2 cloves garlic, minced
¼ tablespoon salt
¼ tablespoon black pepper

FOR THE ARTICHOKE-JALAPEÑO SPREAD:

1 bag store-bought sourdough crisps
or 1 loaf sourdough bread, cut into 24
slivers and lightly oven toasted
1 cup drained and chopped
marinated artichoke hearts
½ cup grated parmesan cheese
4 ounces cream cheese, room temperature
¼ cup Greek yogurt
2 tablespoons chopped jalapeño pepper
¼ tablespoon salt
¼ tablespoon black pepper

KILL LEVEL: Moderate | BODY COUNT: 6 servings | PREP TIME: 5 minutes | COOK AND REST TIME: 23 minutes

1. Brush the steak with 2 tablespoons of the olive oil, and rub with the garlic, salt, and pepper. Let sit.

2. Meanwhile, place 24 sourdough crisps on a platter.

3. Put all the remaining artichoke-jalapeño spread ingredients in a bowl or stand mixer and gently mix until thoroughly combined.

4. Slather the artichoke-jalapeño spread evenly on the sourdough crisps. Any leftover spread can be refrigerated for up to 5 days.

5. Heat a skillet (cast iron if you have it) over medium-high heat until hot, then add the remaining ½ tablespoon of olive oil, swirling to coat. Once the oil is hot, add the steak. Sear the steak on the first side for 4 minutes, or until a brown crust has formed, then flip and cook another 3 to 4 minutes.

6. Transfer the steak to a cutting board and let rest for 5 minutes. Slice very thinly. Thicker slices will be hard to chew.

7. To finish assembling, place the steak slices on top of the spread and serve warm.

THE WHITE NOISE

FOR THE THYME SIMPLE SYRUP:

1 cup water

1 cup granulated sugar

½ cup fresh thyme sprigs

FOR THE WHITE NOISE:

2 ounces gin

2 ounces Thyme Simple Syrup

1 tablespoon lime juice

2 ounces white citrus soda, like Squirt

KILL LEVEL: Moderate | **BODY COUNT:** 1 drink | **PREP TIME:** 5 minutes plus an hour to refrigerate | **COOK TIME:** 10 minutes

TIP: The base of any good simple syrup is 1 part water to 1 part granulated sugar. After that, you can add whatever flavoring you'd like. Just don't change it for this drink.

1. Make the thyme simple syrup by combining the water, sugar, and thyme sprigs in a small pot. Bring to a boil over medium heat and stir constantly until the sugar dissolves. Remove from the heat and let cool. Strain the syrup in an airtight container and place in the refrigerator for at least an hour. Discard the thyme sprigs.

2. For the drink, combine the gin, thyme simple syrup, and lime juice in a shaker over ice. Shake until very cold, then pour into a chilled martini glass. Top with the citrus soda.

DRINKING GAME

Take a drink every time a TV appears on your TV.

MAX'S CRAB SUMMER ROLLS
Refreshing Crab Rolls with a Spicy Peanut Dipping Sauce

FOR THE CRAB SUMMER ROLLS:

4 ounces rice noodles, uncooked

24 (8-inch) round rice paper wrappers

16 ounces imitation crabmeat

½ cucumber, thinly sliced lengthwise

4 ounces matchstick carrots

2 cups fresh mint leaves

2 cups fresh basil leaves

any other fresh ingredients you might enjoy

FOR THE SPICY PEANUT DIPPING SAUCE:

2 tablespoons creamy peanut butter, melted

¼ cup apple cider vinegar

1 tablespoon soy sauce

1 tablespoon minced ginger

2 tablespoons sriracha

1 tablespoon brown sugar

KILL LEVEL: Moderate to hard | **BODY COUNT:** 6 servings | **PREP TIME:** 30 minutes | **COOK TIME:** 5 minutes

TIP: You are going to want to use real lump crabmeat in the summer rolls, but trust me when I say that they work best with imitation crabmeat.

1. Cook the rice noodles according to package directions. Let cool.

2. Fill a large bowl with very hot water. Soak 1 rice paper wrapper at a time for about 10 seconds, or until pliable. Spread the wrapper on a nonstick surface.

3. In the center of the wrapper, sprinkle an even amount of all the summer roll ingredients. Be careful not to overfill or the wrapper could split or not seal.

4. Fold the top and bottom of the wrapper tightly over the filling, then roll up the sides. Repeat with the next wrapper until all 24 are made.

5. To make the spicy peanut dipping sauce, mix together all the ingredients and stir until thoroughly combined.

6. Serve the rolls on a platter with a ramekin full of the spicy peanut sauce. I'd say that the sauce keeps in the refrigerator, but it is so good you probably won't have any left.

THE CROAKER QUEEN

½ cup cran-raspberry juice
2 ounces ruby red grapefruit juice
2 ounces vodka
fresh mint, for garnish

KILL LEVEL: Easy | **BODY COUNT:** 1 drink | **PREP TIME:** 5 minutes

1. Mix all the liquid ingredients together in a cocktail shaker and shake vigorously.

2. Pour into a rocks glass over ice.

3. Garnish with a mint leaf and serve.

DRINKING GAME

Take a drink every time Julie nervously plays with her sleeves.

IDENTITY (2003)

Paris, a sex worker, is one of the standouts in a film full of interesting characters. The film follows her back to her hometown of Frostproof, Florida. As she tends to the soil in her orange grove, she shakily discovers a motel room key buried in the dirt. Maybe it's not over for her.

ORANGE GROVE
Sweet Pickled Orange and Goat Cheese Crostini

FOR THE SWEET PICKLED ORANGES:

4 large oranges, peeled and segmented
1½ cups white wine vinegar
2 whole cinnamon sticks
1 tablespoon whole cloves
2 cups granulated sugar

FOR THE GOAT CHEESE CROSTINI:

24 store-bought crostini
8 ounces spreadable goat cheese
24 sweet pickled orange segments (minimum)
sweet pickled orange syrup, for drizzling

KILL LEVEL: Moderate | BODY COUNT: 6 servings | PREP TIME: 20 minutes | COOK TIME: 2 hours

TIP: In making the sweet pickled oranges, navel oranges work best for peeling and keeping the orange segments intact.

1. Make the sweet pickled oranges in advance. Place the orange segments in a large saucepan and cover with water. Place on the stove over low heat. Add the white wine vinegar, cinnamon sticks, and whole cloves. Simmer uncovered for 1½ hours.

2. Add the granulated sugar and turn up the heat to high. Bring to a boil for 3 minutes, stirring until the sugar dissolves and the syrup begins to thicken. Once the syrup is about as thick as cough syrup, remove from the heat and let cool. Once cool, place in a covered bowl and refrigerate until needed. You don't want to serve the pickled oranges warm.

3. Assemble the crostini on a platter. On each crostino, spread a thick layer of goat cheese and top with 1 orange segment (or more if you have any to spare). Drizzle the crostini with some of the orange syrup and serve.

THE STORM

2 ounces bourbon

2 ounces blackberry liqueur

4 ounces ginger beer

KILL LEVEL: Easy | BODY COUNT: 1 drink | PREP TIME: 5 minutes

1. Add the bourbon and blackberry liqueur to a tall glass filled halfway with ice. Stir.

2. Top with the ginger beer and slowly mix it into the rest of the beverage.

DRINKING GAME

Take a drink every time someone finds or uses a room key.

DAWN OF THE DEAD (2004)

Oh, damn. I'd hate for this to be a spoiler, but who could forget the birth of the zombie baby at the home goods store? Such a tender moment.

ZOMBIE BABY KALE SALAD
Lemony Kale Salad with Roasted Chickpeas and Shaved Parmesan

FOR THE LEMON VINAIGRETTE:

8 tablespoons fresh lemon juice
2 cloves garlic, minced
¼ teaspoon granulated sugar
¼ teaspoon black pepper
¼ cup olive oil

FOR THE ROASTED CHICKPEAS:

1 (16-ounce) can chickpeas, rinsed and drained
2 tablespoons olive oil
¼ teaspoon salt
1 tablespoon cayenne pepper
1 tablespoon garlic powder
1 tablespoon onion powder

FOR THE SALAD:

8 cups baby kale
10 ounces shaved parmesan cheese
Lemon Vinaigrette
Roasted Chickpeas
salt and pepper, to taste

KILL LEVEL: Easy | BODY COUNT: 6 servings |
PREP TIME: 10 minutes | COOK TIME: 45 minutes

1. Make the vinaigrette by whisking together all the ingredients. Let sit to combine.

2. Preheat the oven to 450°F. Allow the chickpeas to dry a bit, but they don't have to be bone-dry. Spread them on a baking sheet. Toss with the olive oil, sprinkle with all the seasonings, and use your clean hands to coat the chickpeas evenly. Bake for approximately 45 minutes, or until crunchy but not burned. Start to keep an eye on them at around 30 minutes. Let cool before adding to the salad.

3. Rinse the kale, shake off excess water, and let dry while the chickpeas are in the oven. Once dry, put it in a large serving bowl. Pour the vinaigrette over the kale and toss to coat evenly. Add the cooled chickpeas and shaved parmesan and toss again. Plate and sprinkle with salt and pepper to taste.

Remember how cool it was when they drenched the zombies
in gasoline and lit them on fire? I mean, who doesn't love fire?
Well, now you can feel like a true zombie hunter with...

THE FLAMING ZOMBIE

1 ounce dark rum

1 ounce light rum

4 ounces pineapple juice

2 ounces orange juice

1 ounce grenadine

1 tablespoon lime juice

1 ounce overproof (flammable) rum

KILL LEVEL: Moderate | **BODY COUNT:** 1 drink | **PREP TIME:** 5 minutes

1. In a cocktail shaker over ice, combine all the ingredients except the overproof rum. Once shaken, pour into a heatproof glass over fresh ice.

2. Slowly drizzle the overproof rum on top of the drink. Use a long match or lighter to light the rum topper on fire. Be careful!

3. Blow out the flame before you drink, silly. Enjoy!

TIP: When drizzling the overproof rum into the glass, it sometimes helps to slowly pour it over the back of a spoon so that it doesn't mix in with the rest of the drink.

DRINKING GAME

Take a drink whenever you hear a curiously different version of a popular song.

CRAWL (2019)

In this modern disaster horror film, a father, his daughter, and their dog are hunted by gators after becoming trapped in a house during a hurricane. This masterful creature feature has more depth than meets the alligator eye.

ALLIGATOR BITES
Cajun Alligator Chunks Served with a Spicy Dipping Sauce

FOR THE DIPPING SAUCE:

1 cup mayo

½ cup Frank's Red Hot Cayenne Pepper Sauce

1 tablespoon chipotle powder

1 tablespoon lemon juice

1 tablespoon apple cider vinegar

salt and pepper, to taste

FOR THE ALLIGATOR:

1 pound alligator, cut into bite-size chunks

½ tablespoon salt, plus more for the flour mixture

½ tablespoon black pepper, plus more for the flour mixture

1 cup buttermilk

¼ cup Frank's Red Hot Cayenne Pepper Sauce

vegetable oil, for frying

2½ cups all-purpose flour

1 tablespoon Old Bay Seasoning

1 teaspoon garlic powder

KILL LEVEL: Moderate | BODY COUNT: 6 servings | PREP TIME: 10 minutes | COOK TIME: 20 minutes

TIP: If your local butcher shop doesn't have alligator, you can always order it online. Although not the real deal, chicken breast will do in a pinch.

1. Make the dipping sauce by thoroughly combining all the ingredients.

2. Season the alligator chunks with salt and pepper, and let sit.

3. In a large bowl, whisk together the buttermilk and Frank's Red Hot. Transfer the alligator chunks to the bowl and coat well. Let marinate for 30 minutes.

4. Heat the vegetable oil in a large pot over medium-high heat.

5. While the oil is heating, line a plate with paper towels. In a wide, shallow bowl, combine the flour, Old Bay, garlic powder, and a dash of salt and pepper.

6. When the oil is crackling hot, dredge a chunk of alligator in the flour mixture. Make sure it is completely covered. Gently place in the hot oil and fry on one side first, then the other, about 5 minutes per side. Do not overcrowd the oil by adding too many chunks at once.

7. When the alligator chunks are golden brown, remove them from the oil and place them on the paper towel–lined plate. Let stand until all the chunks are fried.

8. Serve the alligator bites on a platter with toothpicks and the spicy dipping sauce.

THE CATEGORY 5

2 ounces white rum

2 ounces dark rum

2 ounces passion fruit juice

1 ounce guava juice

½ ounce grenadine

1 tablespoon lime juice

1 maraschino cherry, for garnish

KILL LEVEL: Easy | **BODY COUNT:** 1 drink | **PREP TIME:** 5 minutes

1. Add all the liquid ingredients to a shaker with ice and shake it up.

2. Empty the contents, including the ice, into a hurricane glass.

3. Garnish with a cherry.

DRINKING GAME

Take a drink every time someone in the room jumps out of their seat. Full disclosure, my guests and I got pretty drunk with this game.

THE WICKER MAN (1973)

On the remote island of Summerisle, a young girl goes missing during the annual harvest. The police chief in charge of her case discovers that things might not be as they seem.

HARVEST TARTLETS
Rustic Apple and Persimmon Tarts with Gruyère and Thyme

all-purpose flour, for dusting

3 rolls premade pie dough, like Pillsbury

2 tablespoons unsalted butter

1 small yellow onion, thinly sliced

½ cup crème fraiche

2 teaspoons Dijon mustard

1 cup grated gruyère cheese, divided

2 tablespoons chopped fresh thyme leaves, divided

2 green apples, cored and thinly sliced

1 persimmon, thinly sliced

salt and pepper, to taste

KILL LEVEL: Moderate | BODY COUNT: 6 servings | PREP TIME: 30 minutes | COOK TIME: 1 hour and 10 minutes

TIP: If you don't have pie weights, just line the bottom crust with parchment, cover with uncooked dry beans or rice, and bake. Note that baking this way means you can't cook the beans or rice later. The good news is you can put them into a ziplock bag and use them over and over as pie weights.

1. You'll need 6 individual aluminum pie tins, each measuring 5 inches in diameter, to make these tarts. On a lightly floured surface, roll out the premade pie dough and cut out rounds 6 to 7 inches in diameter. If you don't have a ruler handy, you can use the tops of the pie tins and estimate a cut. Press the dough rounds into the pie tins. (For perspective, you should be able to get around 2 tartlet crusts out of each roll with some dough left over.)

2. Place the tartlet tins in the refrigerator and preheat the oven to 350°F.

3. Once the oven is heated, lay parchment paper at the bottom of each pit crust, then place pie weights on top and bake for 25 minutes. Remove the weights and bake for another 15 minutes.

4. While the pie crusts are cooking, in a skillet over medium heat, melt the butter. Once it is hot, add the onion and cook for about 10 minutes, until caramelized. Remove from the heat.

5. Remove the pie tins from the oven and set aside to cool, but keep the oven on.

6. In a separate bowl, stir together the crème fraiche and mustard. Use a brush to spread the mixture evenly over the inside of the crusts.

7. Sprinkle half of the cheese and thyme into the crusts. Add the apples and persimmon, as well as the caramelized onion. Top with the remaining cheese and thyme, and season with salt and pepper.

8. Bake for another 15 minutes at 350°F. Let cool and serve.

THE BURNING MAN

2 ounces bison grass vodka
2 ounces elderflower liqueur
4 ounces sparkling rosé
blade of grass or wheat, for garnish

1. Add all the liquid ingredients to a red wine glass filled halfway with ice. Give it one slow stir.

2. Garnish with a blade of grass or wheat. Enjoy!

KILL LEVEL: Easy | BODY COUNT: 1 drink | PREP TIME: 5 minutes

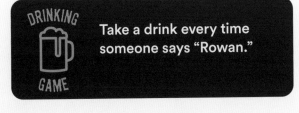

DRINKING GAME

Take a drink every time someone says "Rowan."

28 DAYS LATER (2002)

When the survivors show up at the mansion, the soldiers prepare a feast to celebrate their arrival. Unfortunately, Jones, the soldier in charge of cooking, makes an omelet using expired eggs. Maybe they should have brought some of those irradiated green apples with them.

"A FEAST, JONES"

Omelet Muffins and Homemade Apple Sauce (Who doesn't love breakfast for dinner?)

FOR THE APPLE SAUCE:

4 large green apples, peeled, cored, and roughly chopped

½ cup apple juice

2 tablespoons granulated sugar

2 tablespoons brown sugar

2 tablespoons ground cinnamon

½ tablespoon ground cloves

FOR THE OMELET MUFFINS:

8 large eggs

½ cup heavy cream

1 cup shredded mozzarella cheese

1 head broccoli, roughly chopped

1 cup chopped deli ham

1 cup chopped yellow onion

½ cup grated parmesan cheese

2 cloves garlic, minced

salt and pepper, to taste

KILL LEVEL: Moderate | BODY COUNT: 6 servings | PREP TIME: 25 minutes | COOK TIME: 45 minutes

1. First, make the apple sauce so it has time to cool in the refrigerator. Combine all the ingredients in a saucepan and bring to a boil over medium-high heat. Reduce the heat, cover the pan, and let simmer for about 30 minutes, or until the apples are tender.

2. Remove the lid and simmer for another 5 minutes to thicken the sauce.

3. Mash the apples with a hand potato masher until you reach a consistency that you like. You can always use a blender if you like thin sauce. Chill in the refrigerator until you are ready to serve.

4. In the meantime, preheat the oven to 350°F.

5. In a large bowl, whisk together the eggs and heavy cream. Then stir in all the other ingredients and anything else you might want to add.

6. Grease a 12-cup muffin tin with nonstick spray. Spoon the egg mixture into the cups and fill about two-thirds of the way up. There should be enough batter for about 18 muffins.

7. Bake for 25 minutes, or until the eggs are cooked. You can check by poking the middle of a muffin with a knife. If it comes out clean, the muffin is cooked. As the muffins cool, they will shrink a bit so don't panic.

8. Once the omelet muffins are cool to the touch but still warm, run a knife around the edges of the muffin cups to release the muffins. Serve warm with a side of the apple sauce.

> **TIP:** If you want to alter the omelet muffins recipe, don't forget to precook any raw meats before adding them to the batter or you might end up with a different kind of virus.

THE MONKEY BRAINS SHOT

1 ounce vodka
1 ounce lemon juice
1 ounce Irish cream liqueur
few drops of grenadine

KILL LEVEL: Moderate | BODY COUNT: 1 shot | PREP TIME: 5 minutes

DRINKING GAME

Take a drink every time you see obvious product placement.

1. Chill all the ingredients in the fridge overnight.

2. Add the vodka and lemon juice to the shot glass.

3. Using a food syringe or dropper, slowly drizzle the Irish cream liqueur on the bottom of the shot glass. It will start to form what should look like brains.

4. Add a few drops of grenadine blood and serve!

PIRANHA (1978)

This classic B movie tells the story of a river infested with lethal, genetically altered piranha, threatening the lives of the local inhabitants and the visitors to a nearby summer resort.

PIRANHA SOUP

Seared White Fish in a Garlicky Broth Topped with a Mini Crab Cake

FOR THE MINI CRAB CAKES:

1 large egg

¼ cup mayo

2 tablespoons dried parsley

2 teaspoons Dijon mustard

2 teaspoons Worcestershire sauce

2 teaspoons Old Bay Seasoning

1 teaspoon lemon juice

dash of salt

1 pound fresh lump crabmeat

⅔ cup crumbled saltine crackers

FOR THE SOUP:

4 pounds white fish, like tilapia, cut into chunks

4 cloves garlic, minced

4 tablespoons lime juice

1 tablespoon apple cider vinegar

salt and pepper, to taste

½ cup plus 2 tablespoons olive oil, divided

2 large beefsteak tomatoes, chopped

1 large green pepper, cut into thin strips

1 medium yellow onion, chopped

2 tablespoons chopped green onion, for garnish

2 tablespoons chopped fresh cilantro, for garnish

KILL LEVEL: Hard | BODY COUNT: 6 servings | PREP TIME: 3 hours and 30 minutes | COOK TIME: 45 minutes

1. First, start the crab cakes. Whisk together the egg, mayo, parsley, mustard, Worcestershire sauce, Old Bay Seasoning, lemon juice, and salt in a large bowl. Slowly fold in the crabmeat and then the cracker crumbs. Cover tightly and refrigerate for at least 3 hours.

2. Start the soup. Place the chunks of white fish in a large bowl and season with the garlic, lime juice, apple cider vinegar, and salt and pepper. Let the fish marinate in the refrigerator for 2 hours.

3. In a large saucepan, heat ½ cup of the olive oil over medium-high heat. Add the fish chunks and sear for a few minutes on all sides. Lower the heat and add enough water to fully cover the fish. Bring to a boil and cook for 10 minutes.

4. Remove the fish and broth from the heat. Transfer to a blender or food processor, and blend until smooth. Set aside.

5. Preheat the oven to 450°F. Spray a baking sheet with cooking spray. Remove the crab cake mixture from the refrigerator and portion into 12 mounds on the baking sheet. The mounds should form crab cakes small enough to float on top of the soup. Bake for 12 to 14 minutes, or until lightly browned.

6. In a larger pot, heat the remaining 2 tablespoons of oil over medium-high heat. Add the tomatoes, green pepper, and onion, and cook until the vegetables are soft, approximately 7 minuets. Add the pureed fish broth from the blender or food processor to the pot, and turn down the heat very low.

7. While the soup is heating, remove the crab cakes from the oven.

8. Once the soup is hot enough, serve it in a bowl and top with a mini crab cake. Garnish with green onion and cilantro and serve.

9. Cover leftover crab cakes tightly and refrigerate for up to 5 days or freeze for up to 3 months. You can even make the crab cakes in advance and reheat them in the oven when you are ready to serve the soup.

> **TIP:** Do not bring the piranha soup to a boil once you add the pureed fish broth. It will separate and be very difficult to get back together. Also, if you can get your hands on true piranha meat, go for it! It will cook the same way, but it isn't easy to find.

THE "MAN CANNOT LIVE ON BOOZE ALONE"

1 ounce scotch

1 ounce gin

1 ounce bourbon

1 ounce tequila

4 ounces cola

1 lime wedge, for garnish

1 lemon wedge, for garnish

1. Add all the booze to a shaker with ice. Shake it up.

2. Empty the contents of the shaker, including the ice, into a pint glass. Add the cola.

3. Garnish with a lemon wedge and a lime wedge, and serve!

KILL LEVEL: Easy | BODY COUNT: 1 drink | PREP TIME: 5 minutes

DRINKING GAME

Drink every time there is a camera angle from the piranha's point of view.

DINNER IS
SERVED

THE DESCENT (2005)

This terrifying film follows a group of girlfriends who decide to go spelunking in an unmarked cave in the Appalachian Mountains. Unfortunately for them, the locals they find inside don't have a taste for traditional Appalachian fare like the recipes below.

APPALACHIAN SALAD AND CRAWLER'S CHILI

Wilted Greens in a Warm Bacon Dressing Topped with a Fried Egg
Served with Chorizo and Chicken Brunswick Stew Chili–Style

FOR THE SALAD:

2 pounds mixed greens, like spinach, arugula, or your favorite store bag

½ large red onion, very thinly sliced

½ pound bacon

6 large eggs

¾ cup apple cider vinegar

3 teaspoons brown sugar

1 tablespoon salt

1 teaspoon black pepper

FOR THE CHILI:

6 tablespoons butter, unsalted

1½ medium red onions, chopped

5 cloves garlic, minced

3 large russet potatoes, diced

1 (16-ounce) can lima beans

2 (16-ounce) cans whole kernel corn

3 cups chicken broth or stock

1 (16-ounce) can diced tomatoes

1 pound chorizo links, sliced

1¼ cups smoky barbecue sauce

2 tablespoons Worcestershire sauce

2 tablespoons brown sugar

2 teaspoons salt

1 teaspoon black pepper

1 teaspoon cayenne pepper

3 large boneless, skinless chicken breasts, cooked and chopped (approximately 1.5 pounds)

1. In a large bowl, make the salad by tossing together the greens and onion.

2. Cook the bacon strips in a large frying pan over medium heat, about 13 minutes, or until extra crispy. Remove from the pan and let cool on a paper towel–lined plate. Crumble the bacon when it is cool.

3. Using the bacon grease left in the pan, fry the eggs over easy on medium heat. Remove and set on a plate lightly brushed with cooking oil to prevent sticking. Cover to keep warm.

4. In the same pan over medium heat, stir in the vinegar, brown sugar, salt, and pepper. Stir continuously for 2 minutes to thicken the dressing.

5. Pour the hot dressing over the greens and toss quickly to coat. Sprinkle the bacon crumbles over the greens and toss again.

6. To serve, portion the salad onto individual plates, and top each serving with a fried egg.

7. To make the chili, melt the butter in a large pot over medium heat. Add the onions and cook until translucent, about 10 minutes, stirring frequently. Add the garlic and cook for 2 minutes more.

KILL LEVEL: Moderate | BODY COUNT: 6 servings | PREP TIME: 20 minutes | COOK TIME: 1 hour and 30 minutes

8. Add the potatoes, lima beans, corn, chicken broth, tomatoes, and chorizo. Bring to a boil, then cover the pot, reduce the heat to low, and let simmer for about 30 minutes.

9. Add the barbecue sauce, Worcestershire sauce, brown sugar, salt, black pepper, cayenne pepper, and cooked chicken, and stir thoroughly. Simmer covered for 15 minutes.

10. Uncover and let simmer for another 15 minutes, then serve in individual bowls with the individual plates of salad.

TIP: Traditional Brunswick stew is made with squirrel. While I don't encourage backyard hunting, if you are adventurous enough and can get your hands on some squirrel meat, give it a try. Just make sure it is cooked thoroughly before adding it to the stew in place of or in addition to the chicken.

THE ALBINO ANIMAL

2 ounces vodka

2 ounces anisette liqueur

1 ounce triple sec

1 tablespoon lime juice

drop of bitters

1. Add all the booze and the lime juice to a shaker with ice. Shake it up.

2. Empty the contents of the shaker into a rocks glass. Carefully add a drop of bitters into the glass, swirl the ice, and serve!

KILL LEVEL: Easy | BODY COUNT: 1 drink | PREP TIME: 5 minutes

DRINKING GAME

Take a drink every time you spot a monster hidden in the caves.

SCREAM 2 (1997)

In the opening sequence, Maureen and Phil are discussing the movie that they are going to see. Maureen is not thrilled about seeing a "white" movie, so Phil jokes, "tonight we're going to have an all-black movie—all-black cast, all-black wardrobe, black eyes, black everything...black-eyed peas!"

PHIL'S BLACK-EYED PEA SOUP
Hearty Black-Eyed Pea and Cheese Tortellini Soup

16 ounces dried black-eyed peas
2 tablespoons butter
1 medium yellow onion, chopped
6 cloves garlic, minced
8 cups chicken broth
1 cup water
1 cup dry red wine, like merlot
1 (28-ounce) can diced tomatoes
2 teaspoons black pepper
1 teaspoon salt
1 teaspoon red pepper flakes
2 tablespoons chopped fresh basil
24 ounces frozen cheese tortellini
16 ounces frozen spinach
1½ cups grated parmesan cheese

1. Prepare the black-eyed peas according to package directions. Cover and set aside until needed.

2. Melt the butter in a large pot over medium heat. Add the onion and garlic and cook for about 5 minutes over medium heat. Stir in the chicken broth, water, wine, tomatoes, and seasonings, and bring to a boil.

3. Add the frozen tortellini, frozen spinach, and prepared black-eyed peas. Reduce the heat and simmer uncovered for about 25 minutes, stirring frequently.

4. Remove from the heat and add the parmesan cheese, stirring well. Serve hot in large individual soup bowls.

KILL LEVEL: Easy | BODY COUNT: 6 servings |
PREP TIME: 10 minutes | COOK TIME: 35 minutes

TIP: If you plan on using precooked canned black-eyed peas for the soup, make sure they are not seasoned and to drain and rinse them very well.

THE DEBBIE SALTED APPLE CIDER MARTINI

2 ounces vodka

4 ounces store-bought apple cider

½ teaspoon pink salt

1 cinnamon stick or apple slice, for garnish

KILL LEVEL: Easy | BODY COUNT: 1 drink | PREP TIME: 5 minutes.

1. Add the vodka, cider, and salt to a shaker with ice. Shake it up until it's cold.

2. Strain the contents into a chilled martini glass.

3. Garnish with a cinnamon stick or apple slice, or both, and serve extra cold.

DRINKING GAME

Take a drink every time one of the characters from the original gets attacked.

STIR OF ECHOES (1999)

In the film, phone operator Tom Witzky begins experiencing a series of frightening, ghostly visions after insisting he be hypnotized by his sister-in-law.

TOM'S HYPNOTIC GHOST PEPPER CURRY

Chicken Curry with Chopped Ghost Peppers and Jasmine Rice

2 tablespoons olive oil

2 pounds boneless, skinless chicken thighs, chopped into 1-inch chunks

¾ cup chopped dried ghost pepper

2 medium yellow onions, chopped

5 cloves garlic, minced

1 cup chopped green onion

2 tablespoons curry powder

3 tablespoons red curry paste

2 tablespoons minced fresh ginger

1 tablespoon smoked paprika

2 (14-ounce) cans full-fat coconut milk

salt and black pepper, to taste

3 cups cooked jasmine rice

chopped cilantro, for garnish (optional)

lime wedges, for garnish (optional)

KILL LEVEL: Moderate | BODY COUNT: 6 servings | PREP TIME: 10 minutes | COOK TIME: 35 minutes

1. Heat a large wok to medium-high heat and add the olive oil. Once hot, add the chicken, ghost pepper, and yellow onions. Cook for 8 to 10 minutes, or until the onions and pepper are soft and the chicken is mostly cooked through.

2. Add the garlic and green onion and cook for another 2 minutes, stirring frequently.

3. Add the curry powder, curry paste, ginger, and paprika. Stir for about a minute.

4. Add the coconut milk and bring to a boil. Reduce the heat and let simmer for about 15 minutes. Add salt and black pepper to your liking.

5. Serve the curry in individual bowls over cooked jasmine rice (that you already prepared following package instructions), and garnish with chopped cilantro and lime wedges, if using.

TIP: Ghost pepper goes a long way, so be careful you don't add too much. Also, the jasmine rice can be prepared up to 3 days in advance and kept in the fridge so it's ready for you when you need it.

THE PAINT IT BLACK

2 tablespoons maraschino cherry juice from the jar

5 drops of black food coloring

2 ounces vodka

½ cup orange juice

KILL LEVEL: Moderate | BODY COUNT: 1 drink | PREP TIME: 5 minutes

1. Mix the cherry juice and black food coloring in a small bowl (preferably not plastic, as it could stain). Set aside.

2. Fill a rocks glass to the brim with ice. Add the vodka and orange juice. Give it a stir and let it settle.

3. Slowly drizzle the black cherry juice on top of the ice using the back of a spoon. You should be able to watch the juice "paint" the bright drink black.

DRINKING GAME

Why not? Take a drink every time you hear "Paint It Black." If you don't know the song, be sure to listen to it before you watch the movie.

BROKEN LIZARD'S CLUB DREAD (2004)

This one speaks for itself, right? I mean, the secret ingredient. Coconut Pete's paella? *Coconut* Pete's Paella? *COCONUT!* Yes, dammit, yes!

COCONUT PETE'S PAELLA

Shrimp and Chorizo Paella Topped with Mussels and Coconut Pete's Special Ingredient

9 cups chicken broth

4 tablespoons olive oil

1 pound chorizo links, sliced

1 medium yellow onion, minced

1 green pepper, chopped

1 red pepper, chopped

4 cloves garlic, minced

1 cup dry white wine, like pinot gris

1 (14-ounce) can diced tomatoes

1 (14-ounce) package baker's coconut

3 cups yellow Spanish rice, uncooked

½ teaspoon saffron threads

salt and black pepper, to taste

1 pound frozen shrimp, thawed, uncooked, deveined, and deshelled

1 pound fresh mussels in the shell

lemon wedges, for garnish

KILL LEVEL: Hard | BODY COUNT: 6 servings | PREP TIME: 10 minutes | COOK TIME: 1 hour

1. Preheat the oven to 400°F. Bring the chicken broth to a boil in a large pot, then reduce the heat to simmer.

2. Meanwhile, in a paella pan, large cast-iron skillet, or oven-safe wok, heat the olive oil over medium-high heat. Add the chorizo and cook until lightly browned, about 1 minute per side. Remove and set aside.

3. Add the onion, green and red peppers, and garlic to the same pan, and cook for about 5 minutes, or until soft. Add the wine, tomatoes, and baker's coconut and stir to combine.

4. Add the rice and saffron to the pan, then pour in 8 cups of the simmering chicken broth and bring to a boil, stirring constantly. Once it starts to aggressively boil, remove the paella pan from the heat.

5. Season with salt and pepper, and arrange the chorizo, shrimp, and mussels on top of the rice.

6. Place the paella pan in the oven and bake uncovered for 25 minutes, or until all of the liquid is absorbed, the rice is tender but not soft, and the mussels have opened. Once the paella goes into the oven, do not stir.

7. Remove the paella from the oven. Add the final cup of broth and bake for another 10 minutes.

8. Remove from the oven and let stand for 5 minutes, covered. Serve in individual bowls with lemon wedges.

> **TIP:** If your mussels don't open, don't try to pry them open and eat them. They were dead from the start and unsafe to eat. If your mussels are open before cooking, they most likely died during the freezing process and are completely safe to eat. If you are using fresh mussels instead, give any open mussels a quick tap on the shell. If they close, they are still alive and okay to consume. If they don't close, they are already dead and should be discarded.

THE PIÑA COLADABURG

1 liter piña colada mix
1 (750-ml) bottle coconut vodka
1 (750-ml) bottle whipped cream vodka
1 (12-ounce) can pineapple juice

1. Mix it all together in a large punch bowl. Serve it over ice. Pretend you are on a tropical island.

KILL LEVEL: Easy | BODY COUNT: 1 large batch (you'll want it for later) | PREP TIME: 5 minutes

DRINKING GAME

Take a drink every time the signature ominous sound effect kicks in. You'll know what I mean when you watch.

PSYCHO (1960)

Marion is tired of sneaking around and having nooners with an unavailable man. She wants to have a respectable dinner date, at home with her mother's picture on the mantle and her sister broiling a steak for three.

MARION'S RESPECTABLE DATE NIGHT
Broiled New York Strip Steak with Mashed Potatoes and Steamed Veggies

FOR THE MASHED POTATOES:

3 pounds russet potatoes, peeled and chopped into 1-inch cubes

3 tablespoons butter

1 cup milk

½ cup sour cream

1 tablespoon garlic powder

salt and black pepper, to taste

FOR THE STEAMED VEGGIES:

3 pounds veggies of your choice, fresh or frozen

FOR THE BROILED STEAK:

6 (8-ounce) New York strip steaks

garlic powder, to taste

salt and black pepper, to taste

6 tablespoons butter

KILL LEVEL: Moderate | BODY COUNT: 6 servings | PREP TIME: 25 minutes | COOK TIME: 50 minutes

1. To make the mashed potatoes, place a large pot of water over medium-high heat.

2. Once the water comes to a rolling boil, add the potatoes and cook for about 15 minutes, until a fork can easily poke through the cubes.

3. Drain the water from the cooked potatoes over a strainer.

4. In the same pot with the hot potato chunks, add the butter, milk, sour cream, garlic powder, and salt and pepper. Mash with a hand mixer or hand potato masher, then cover until ready to serve.

5. To make the steamed veggies, chop all the veggies into bite-size pieces, unless they already come that way.

6. Add 1 inch of water to a saucepan and insert a steamer basket. The surface of the water should be below the basket.

7. Bring the water to a boil over high heat and add the vegetables. Cover the saucepan and reduce the heat to medium.

8. Steam the veggies. Not all veggies cook at the same speed—softer veggies will cook faster than harder ones. If your broccoli finishes before your carrots, it's okay to remove them first. The veggies are done when tender and a fork is able to poke through with ease. Cover and set aside until ready to serve.

9. To make the broiled steak, rub all sides of the steaks with the garlic powder and salt and pepper.

10. Turn the broiler on high and place the steaks on a broiler pan or rimmed baking sheet.

11. Broil the steaks on one side, about 4 to 6 inches from the heat, for 5 minutes.

12. Use tongs to flip the steaks. Place 1 tablespoon of butter on top of each steak and place back in the broiler for another 5 minutes. The internal temperature should be at least 135°F.

13. Remove the steaks from the broiler and plate them. If you have extra pan juices, drizzle some on top of the steaks. Serve with the mashed potatoes and steamed veggies.

> **TIP:** If you don't have a steamer basket, you can always buy steam-in-bag vegetables from your local grocery store and follow the package cooking instructions. Microwaving is another great option. Just place your veggies in a microwave-safe dish and cook on high for approximately 6 minutes.

THE MAMA'S BOY MARTINI

FOR THE SUGAR SNAP PEA–INFUSED VODKA (BATCH):

2 cups chopped sugar snap peas

3 cups vodka

FOR THE MINT SIMPLE SYRUP (BATCH):

2 cups water

2 cups granulated sugar

2 cups fresh mint leaves

FOR THE MAMA'S BOY MARTINI:

4 ounces Sugar Snap Pea–Infused Vodka

1 ounce Mint Simple Syrup

1 ounce club soda

fresh mint leaves, for garnish

KILL LEVEL: Hard | **BODY COUNT:** 1 batch | **PREP TIME:** 1 hour

DRINKING GAME

Take a drink every time Norman mentions birds or taxidermy.

1. To make the Sugar Snap Pea–Infused Vodka, combine the chopped peas and the vodka, and let sit in the fridge overnight or up to 3 days, stirring occasionally.

2. Strain through a cheesecloth and return to the fridge until needed.

3. To make the Mint Simple Syrup, bring the water to a boil over medium heat.

4. Add the sugar and mint leaves. Stir until the sugar is dissolved.

5. Let cool for 30 minutes. Strain the syrup in an airtight container and place in the refrigerator until needed.

6. To make the martini, add the sugar snap pea–infused vodka and mint simple syrup to a shaker with ice. Shake until very cold.

7. Pour into a chilled martini glass and top with the club soda. Garnish with fresh mint and serve.

"THERE'S AN *I* IN *MEAT PIE*"

Traditional Steak and Ale Pie Served with a Slice of Fried Gold (Fried Mac 'N' Cheese)

FOR THE FRIED MAC 'N' CHEESE:

1 pound elbow macaroni

6 tablespoons butter, divided

¼ cup plus 2 tablespoons all-purpose flour

4 cups whole milk, room temperature

¾ tablespoon Dijon mustard

4½ cups grated cheddar cheese or Velveeta, room temperature

salt and black pepper, divided

6 large eggs, beaten

2 cups (or more if you'd like) panko breadcrumbs

vegetable oil, for frying

FOR THE PIE PASTRY:

3 cups all-purpose flour, plus more for dusting

½ teaspoon salt

1 cup butter, chilled and cubed

½ cup water, extra cold

1 large egg, beaten

1. To make the fried mac 'n' cheese, in a large pot of boiling water, cook the macaroni al dente according to package instructions and drain.

2. You can reuse the same pot for this step. Melt 5 tablespoons of the butter over medium heat. Once melted, whisk in the flour and stir frequently until mixed in, about 2 minutes.

3. Slowly add the milk and continue to whisk constantly. Keep whisking until the mixture begins to boil, about 5 minutes. Reduce the heat and simmer until the sauce is thick, about 10 minutes.

4. Remove from the heat and add the remaining tablespoon of butter, as well as the mustard and cheese. Stir until melted and smooth. Season with salt and pepper to taste.

5. Add the cooked macaroni and stir to combine.

6. Spoon the mixture onto a parchment-lined, rimmed baking sheet and smooth it evenly across the sheet. Place it in the refrigerator overnight or until firm, at least 8 hours.

7. Once firm, remove from the fridge and flip the baking sheet over. Peel off the parchment paper and cut into rectangles or whatever shape you'd like.

FOR THE PIE FILLING:

1 tablespoon olive oil

1 tablespoon butter

2 pounds beef chuck steak, cubed

2 large carrots, peeled and chopped

1 medium yellow onion, chopped

4 cloves garlic, minced

1 tablespoon tomato paste

2½ tablespoons Worcestershire sauce

2 tablespoons all-purpose flour

1 cup dark English ale or stout, like Guinness

¼ cup beef stock

1 teaspoon chopped fresh thyme

1 teaspoon salt

2 teaspoons black pepper

KILL LEVEL: Hard | BODY COUNT: 6 servings | PREP TIME: 30 minutes plus 8 hours for dough to set | COOK TIME: 2 hours and 20 minutes

> **TIP:** I suggest making the pie crust and the mac 'n' cheese ahead of time so they are ready to go on the day of your horror movie night. It will make your life easier.

8. Whisk the eggs in a medium shallow bowl, and spread the panko breadcrumbs onto a plate. Season the breadcrumbs with a dash of salt and pepper.

9. Dip the rectangles in the egg, then roll in the panko. Coat completely and set aside.

10. Heat the oil in a saucepan over medium heat until shimmering. Add rectangles to the pan in a single layer, but give them room. Turn occasionally until all sides are brown, about 4 minutes per side. Transfer to a paper towel–lined plate and let rest. Repeat the process until all the rectangles are cooked. Keep covered and warm until ready to serve.

11. To make the pie pastry, add the flour, salt, and butter to a food processor. Pulse until the texture is like coarse breadcrumbs.

12. Turn the processor to the slowest setting, and add the cold water slowly until it begins to form a ball. Feel free to add more or less water as needed. You don't want the dough to be too wet.

13. Remove the ball and wrap it in plastic wrap. Refrigerate until ready to use.

14. To make the pie filling, add the olive oil and butter to a large pot over medium heat. Once hot, add the beef and cook until browned on all sides, approximately 7 to 10 minutes. Remove the meat and set aside.

15. To the same pan, add the carrots and onion and cook until soft, about 6 minutes. Add the garlic, tomato paste, and Worcestershire sauce. Stir to mix well and cook for 1 minute.

16. Sprinkle in the flour and stir until well mixed. Cook for another minute, then add the English ale. Stir until the mixture is well combined and begins to thicken.

17. Add all the remaining ingredients. Add the beef back to the pot, stir, cover, and let simmer for 30 minutes.

18. Remove the lid and let simmer for another 15 minutes. The pie filling should thicken even more. If you need to let it simmer uncovered for a bit longer, that's okay. Just be sure to stir so it doesn't burn.

19. Preheat the oven to 425°F and lightly butter a 9-inch pie pan.

20. Remove the dough from the refrigerator and cut it in half. Set one-half aside and roll out the other half on a lightly floured surface. Cut out a circle about ½ inch larger than your pie pan. Place it into the pan and allow the edges to hang over.

21. Poke holes into the bottom of the crust, then use pie weights, dried beans, or uncooked rice to weigh down the dough. Blind-bake the crust for 15 minutes, or until the edges are golden brown.

22. Meanwhile, roll out the other half of the dough on a floured surface and cut into a 10-inch circle.

23. Remove the baked crust from the oven and add the filling.

24. Brush the edges of both crusts with the beaten egg, then place the uncooked crust, egg wash side down, onto the baked crust. Pinch the edges with a fork to seal the pie.

25. Brush the top of the pie crust with the rest of the beaten egg and cut a few slits into the center of the crust.

26. Bake for 20 minutes, or until golden brown, then cut into 6 large slices and serve with a few slices of the fried mac 'n' cheese.

THE WINCHESTER

1 ounce apple brandy, chilled

1 ounce DeKuyper Pucker Sour Apple Schnapps Liqueur, chilled

12 ounces Hefeweizen beer

KILL LEVEL: Easy | **BODY COUNT:** 1 drink | **PREP TIME:** 5 minutes

1. Pour the apple brandy and sour apple into a pint glass.

2. Slowly add the beer, pouring down the side of the glass, so that all of the ingredients blend nicely. Serve cold. You can add ice if you want to, but I don't recommend it. Just drink it before it gets warm.

DRINKING GAME

Take a drink every time a household item is used as a weapon. Yes, records count.

CUJO (1983)

Dogs eat food out of a bowl, silly. Although, in the movie, Cujo tries to eat the people in the Pinto. Why? Because he was bitten by a bat in a rabbit hole. See what I did there?

THE DOG BOWL
Crispy Burrito Bowl with Stewed Pinto Beans, Rice, and Mexican-style Rabbit

FOR THE BURRITO BOWLS:
6 flour tortillas
2 cups white rice, uncooked

FOR THE PINTO BEANS:
2 (16-ounce) cans pinto beans
2 medium yellow onions, halved
4 cloves garlic, halved
salt and black pepper, to taste

FOR THE MEXICAN-STYLE RABBIT:
2 pounds boneless rabbit loin
1 (28-ounce) can red chile sauce
1 medium yellow onion, chopped
1 jalapeño pepper, chopped
2 cloves garlic, chopped
any other items you would like
to serve with the bowls

KILL LEVEL: Moderate | BODY COUNT: 6 servings |
PREP TIME: 15 minutes | COOK TIME: 8 to 10 hours

1. Preheat the oven to 350°F. You'll need 6 tortilla bowl molds (you can buy online). Place the flour tortillas firmly into the molds and bake for approximately 12 minutes, or until golden brown. Remove from the molds and set aside.

2. To a large pot, add the pinto beans, onions, garlic, and salt and pepper. Pour in enough water (or liquid from the cans of beans) to thoroughly cover the contents of the pot. Bring to a boil, then let simmer for 1 hour, or until soft.

3. Once the beans are soft, discard the onions and garlic, and transfer the beans to a serving bowl. The beans can be made in advance and reheated when needed.

4. Spray the bottom of a slow cooker with cooking spray. Add all the ingredients for the rabbit and cook on low for 8 to 10 hours, until you can easily shred the meat.

5. Toward the end of the rabbit cook time, begin cooking the white rice according to package directions so the rice will be warm and fluffy when the rabbit finishes cooking.

6. Once everything is ready to go, serve the meal buffet-style. Let the guests choose what they want to add to their own burrito bowl: rabbit, rice, beans, guacamole, cilantro, lettuce, sour cream, you name it. Whatever you want to put out for your guests. There is no wrong answer!

TIP: If you don't have a slow cooker, place the Mexican-style rabbit ingredients into an ovenproof dish. Preheat the oven to 325°F. Cover the food with a lid or heavy-duty aluminum foil, and cook for 2 to 2½ hours.

THE RABBIT HOLE

FOR THE MINT SIMPLE SYRUP (BATCH):

1 cup water

1 cup granulated sugar

1 cup fresh mint leaves

FOR THE RABBIT HOLE:

1 ounce carrot juice

2 ounces gin

1 ounce Mint Simple Syrup

2 ounces ginger beer

mint leaves or carrot tops, for garnish

KILL LEVEL: Easy | BODY COUNT: 1 drink |
PREP TIME: 5 minutes | COOK TIME: 30 minutes

1. To make a batch of the mint simple syrup, combine the water, sugar, and mint leaves in a small saucepan. Bring to a boil over medium heat, stirring until the sugar dissolves. Simmer for 1 minute on medium heat. Remove from the heat and let the syrup steep, about 30 minutes. Strain into a jar and place in the fridge to chill until needed.

2. To make the drink, add the carrot juice, gin, and simple syrup to a cocktail shaker over ice. Shake until cold and pour into a rocks glass over fresh ice. Top with the ginger beer. Garnish with mint leaves or carrot tops and serve.

DRINKING GAME

Take a drink every time glass breaks.

HALLOWEEN (1978)

The iconic title sequence of the original *Halloween* (the only version you need to watch) shows a smiling and sparkling jack-o'-lantern, a fine contrast to the horror that is to follow.

JACK-O'-LANTERN BITES
Pumpkin Ravioli in a Brown Butter Sauce with Toasted Pecans

FOR THE RAVIOLI DOUGH:

5 cups all-purpose flour, plus more for dusting

1 teaspoon salt

4 large eggs

1 cup hot water

FOR THE PUMPKIN FILLING:

8 ounces canned pumpkin puree, not spiced

2 tablespoons brown sugar

½ teaspoon nutmeg

½ teaspoon ground cloves

1 teaspoon ground cinnamon

salt and black pepper, to taste

FOR THE BROWN BUTTER SAUCE:

½ cup toasted and crushed pecans

4 ounces butter

2 tablespoons balsamic vinegar

2 tablespoons brown sugar

KILL LEVEL: Hard | BODY COUNT: 6 servings | PREP TIME: 40 minutes plus 1 hour for the dough to rest | COOK TIME: 45 minutes

1. To make the ravioli dough, in a large bowl, mix the flour with the salt.

2. In a medium bowl, whisk the eggs and water until well blended.

3. Slowly add the egg mixture to the flour mixture until well incorporated. Knead the dough until firm. You don't want it too wet, too sticky, or too dry. Roll the dough into a ball and wrap it in plastic wrap. Let it rest at room temperature for at least an hour.

4. While the dough rests, make the pumpkin filling by placing all the ingredients for the filling into a pot over medium heat. Stir to combine, but don't allow the mixture to come to a boil. You want to burn off some of the liquid, so do not cover the pot. Heat for 10 to 12 minutes, or until most of the liquid has evaporated.

5. For the next steps, use a ravioli mold with 12 holes, although a cookie cutter or the top of a ramekin will work just as well. (If using a cookie cutter or ramekin top, it should be 2 to 2½ inches in diameter.) When the dough is ready, divide it into 4 parts and roll them all out on a floured surface using a rolling pin. You want the dough to be very thin. You don't want it to stick to the surface, so lift it up every now and then as you roll.

6. Flour the ravioli mold and place the first layer on the mold so that it covers all 12 holes.

7. Fill the 12 indentations with the pumpkin mixture, being careful not to overfill.

8. Place the next layer of dough on top, and roll the rolling pin over the mold to cut the ravioli. You should have extra dough on the sides. Flip the mold to release the ravioli.

9. Repeat until you have made at least 24 ravioli.

10. Bring a large pot of water to a boil. Boil the ravioli for 5 minutes, then drain and set aside as you make the sauce.

11. For the sauce, first toast the pecans in an oven preheated to 350°F. Let them cool and place them in a ziplock bag. Crush the pecans with a rolling pin or meat hammer. Be careful not to damage whatever surface you are using.

12. Melt the butter in a large skillet over medium heat. Cook for about 4 minutes, or until the butter begins to just brown. Remove from the heat and add the balsamic vinegar and brown sugar. Stir to combine.

13. Add the ravioli to the skillet and spoon the sauce over them to coat. You can do this in batches if all the ravioli don't fit at once.

14. Transfer the coated ravioli to plates and top with the toasted pecans.

THE MICHAEL MYERS MARTINI

FOR THE PEPPERED SIMPLE SYRUP (BATCH):

1½ cups water

1½ cups granulated sugar

2 tablespoons whole white peppercorns

2 tablespoons ground white pepper

4 tablespoons clear vanilla extract

6 sprigs fresh thyme

FOR THE MARTINI:

1 ounce Peppered Simple Syrup

3 ounces vodka

2 teaspoons lemon juice

white peppercorns, for garnish

fresh thyme, for garnish

KILL LEVEL: Moderate | **BODY COUNT:** 1 drink | **PREP TIME:** 5 minutes | **COOK TIME:** 10 minutes

DRINKING GAME

Take a drink every time you hear John Carpenter's iconic theme music.

1. For the peppered simple syrup, combine all the ingredients in a saucepan and place over medium heat. Bring to a boil, then remove and let steep for 30 minutes.

2. Using cheesecloth or a strainer, strain into a jar and place in the fridge until cool.

3. Once the syrup has cooled, add all the liquid ingredients for the martini to a shaker over ice. Shake until really cold and pour into a chilled martini glass.

4. Garnish with white peppercorns and fresh thyme.

CONTAGION (2011)

Did we not just live through this movie? I mean, damn. How accurate was this?
At least Beth had one last night of fun before she ended up...well, you know.

BETH'S NIGHT OUT
Chinese Pork with Rice Noodles and Bok Choy

3 pounds pork tenderloin

6 tablespoons honey

6 tablespoons hoisin sauce

4 tablespoons soy sauce

2 tablespoons oyster sauce

4 tablespoons minced ginger

2 tablespoons sesame oil

2 teaspoons Chinese five spice

salt and black pepper, to taste

3 large heads bok choy, chopped

2 (32-ounce) packages beef broth

16 ounces rice noodles, uncooked

chopped green onions, for garnish
(just the green sections)

KILL LEVEL: Moderate | BODY COUNT: 6 servings |
PREP TIME: 10 minutes | COOK TIME: 35 minutes

1. Preheat the oven to 425°F. Cut the pork tenderloin in half lengthwise and poke the meat all over with a fork.

2. Create a sauce by whisking the honey, hoisin sauce, soy sauce, oyster sauce, ginger, sesame oil, and five spice. Rub 2 tablespoons of the marinade onto the pork.

3. Place the tenderloin on a roasting pan or rimmed baking sheet and roast in the oven for approximately 10 minutes. Then brush the pork with 3 more tablespoons of the marinade and roast for another 20 minutes, or until the center reaches 145°F. Sprinkle with salt and pepper to taste.

4. Meanwhile, bring a medium pot of water to a boil and add the bok choy. Cook for approximately 1 minute, or until the leaves are tender.

5. In a separate large pot, bring the beef broth to a boil and cook the rice noodles in the broth according to the package instructions. (You will be using the broth in place of any other liquids the instructions require.)

6. Remove the cooked pork from the oven, then let it rest for 5 minutes before thinly slicing.

7. In individual large bowls, add the noodles with broth, then arrange the pork and bok choy on top. Drizzle each bowl with an even amount of the remaining marinade and top with the scallions.

TIP: I like to make extra marinade for the noodles and keep it as a sauce for later. It's great on other meats and vegetables and will last in the fridge for about a week.

THE PANDEMIC

3 ounces banana liqueur

1 ounce scotch

1 ounce sherry

1 tablespoon lime juice

1 tablespoon ginger syrup (from the pickled ginger jar)

dash of angostura bitters

pickled ginger slices, for garnish

1. Mix all the liquids together in a cocktail shaker. Serve over ice. Garnish with a few slices of pickled ginger.

2. Try to pretend the pandemic didn't happen.

3. Never watch *Contagion* again.

KILL LEVEL: Easy | BODY COUNT: 1 drink | PREP TIME: 5 minutes

DRINKING GAME

Take a drink every time you experience déjà vu from basically living this movie.

THE RUINS (2008)

Based on an equally awesome best-selling book, this strange supernatural flick leaves its leads stranded on the ruins of a Mayan temple. Unlike our heroes, we'll have plenty to eat as we watch.

A MEAL FIT FOR THE MAYANS

Traditional Mayan Fare: Cochinita Pibil over Quinoa with a Side of Deconstructed Street Corn and Topped with Pickled Onions

FOR THE COCHINITA PIBIL:

3 pounds pork shoulder

1 cup orange juice

½ cup lime juice

3 ounces red achiote paste

¼ cup chopped cilantro

3 cups quinoa, uncooked

cotija cheese, for garnish

lime wedges, for garnish

FOR THE DECONSTRUCTED STREET CORN:

2 (16-ounce) cans whole kernel corn

¼ cup mayo

½ cotija cheese

1 lime, juiced

½ tablespoon red pepper flakes

¼ cup minced fresh cilantro

1 large red onion, diced

1. To make the cochinita pibil, place the pork shoulder in a slow cooker with the orange juice, lime juice, achiote paste, and cilantro. Cook on low for about 10 hours, or until the pork can be shredded.

2. Toward the end of cook time, prepare the quinoa according to package directions and keep warm.

3. For the street corn, first dry and then char the canned kernels in a cast-iron pan (the cast iron is optional). Then combine the charred corn and the other ingredients in a large bowl, mix thoroughly, and refrigerate for at least an hour. The street corn should be served cold.

FOR THE PICKLED ONIONS:

½ cup water

¼ cup apple cider vinegar

¼ cup white vinegar

1 tablespoon granulated sugar

1 teaspoon salt

½ teaspoon honey

2 tablespoons red pepper flakes

1 large red onion, very thinly sliced

KILL LEVEL: Easy | BODY COUNT: 6 servings | PREP TIME: 10 minutes plus 2 hours to refrigerate | COOK TIME: 8 to 10 hours

4. While you are waiting for the pork to cook, make the pickled onions by placing a medium-size pot over high heat. Add the water, vinegars, sugar, salt, honey, and red pepper flakes and bring to a boil, stirring occasionally. Once it boils, remove from the stove and add the onion. Pour all the contents into a sealable jar or storage container, and refrigerate for at least 2 hours (or overnight if you decide to make it in advance).

5. To serve, place the quinoa on a plate and top it with the shredded pork shoulder. Sprinkle with cotija cheese, then serve with pickled onions and lime wedges. Add some deconstructed street corn to the plate and enjoy!

TIP: If you don't have a slow cooker, place the cochinita pibil ingredients in an ovenproof dish lined with banana leaves (optional). Preheat the oven to 300°F. Cover the food with a lid or heavy-duty aluminum foil and cook for approximately 4 hours.

THE UNDER THE MEXICAN SUN

3 jalapeño peppers, divided
2 cups tequila
2 cups organic margarita mix
2 cups guava juice
1 lime, cut into small wedges
salt for the rim (optional)

KILL LEVEL: Easy | BODY COUNT: Small batch | PREP TIME: 10 minutes plus overnight to refrigerate

DRINKING GAME
Take a drink every time the flowers talk.

1. Slice 2 of the peppers lengthwise and add them to a pitcher with all the liquid ingredients. If you like heat, keep the seeds. If not, remove them. Cover and place in the refrigerator overnight.

2. Rub a small lime wedge around the rim of each glass and add the salt if you choose. Then add ice and the cold margarita.

3. Thinly slice the last pepper and float some on top of each drink. Enjoy!

SWEET TOOTH

EVENT HORIZON (1997)

In this sci-fi cult classic, the ship's crew has to bend space and time by creating a black hole to travel through to track down a lost spaceship.

THE BLACK HOLE
Dark Chocolate Espresso Mousse Crusted with Caramelized Sugar

8 ounces dark chocolate, chips or squares

3 large egg yolks

2 tablespoons instant espresso granules

9 tablespoons granulated sugar, divided

2 cups heavy cream, divided

KILL LEVEL: Moderate | **BODY COUNT:** 6 servings | **PREP TIME:** 10 minutes plus 2.5 hours to refrigerate | **COOK TIME:** 2 minutes

TIP: If you don't have a brûlée torch, a grill lighter will work, although it will take longer and might melt the mousse a little bit. I don't recommend using the broiler. You will end up with a crusty milkshake.

1. In a large microwave-safe bowl, melt the chocolate in 30-second increments in the microwave. Be careful not to burn it. If it looks like it is almost melted, you can give it a stir to make sure.

2. In a saucepan, whisk together the egg yolks, espresso granules, 6 tablespoons of the sugar, and 1 cup of the heavy cream. Cook over medium heat, constantly stirring, for 2 minutes, or until everything is completely blended.

3. Add the mixture to the bowl of melted chocolate and whisk until there are no lumps. Refrigerate for at least 30 minutes.

4. Beat the remaining 1 cup of heavy cream until stiff and fold it into the chilled chocolate mixture.

5. Divide the mousse into ramekins and refrigerate for at least 2 hours.

6. Remove the mousse cups from the fridge and sprinkle the remaining 3 tablespoons of sugar evenly over the top. Using a brûlée torch, crystallize the sugar on top until it is solid. You should be able to tap it lightly with a butter knife without cracking it.

Dr. Weir has developed an experimental gravity drive. The crew will use this instrument to generate an artificial black hole to bridge two points in space-time, reducing travel time over astronomical distances.

THE GRAVITY DRIVE

2 ounces Patrón XO Cafe
2 ounces butterscotch liqueur
2 ounces cold black coffee

KILL LEVEL: Easy | BODY COUNT: 1 drink | PREP TIME: 5 minutes

1. Mix all the ingredients together in a shaker, pour in a rocks glass over ice, and serve!

DRINKING GAME

Take a drink every time someone says Dr. Weir's name.

THE EVIL DEAD (1981)

Sam Raimi's horror classic was made successfully on a very small budget. In fact, the crew used milk, corn syrup, and creamed corn for most of their gore effects.

ZOMBIE GUTS COOKIES
Green Creamed Corn and Salted Caramel Cookies

1 (14-ounce) can creamed corn

2 tablespoons heavy cream

½ cup granulated sugar

¼ cup brown sugar

½ cup butter, softened

½ teaspoon salt

1 large egg

2 cups all-purpose flour

½ teaspoon baking soda

½ teaspoon baking powder

20 drops of green food coloring

8 ounces caramel chips

KILL LEVEL: Moderate | BODY COUNT: 6 servings | PREP TIME: 10 minutes plus 1.5 hours to chill | COOK TIME: 25 minutes

1. In a saucepan over medium heat, combine the creamed corn, heavy cream, and sugars. Cook until thickened, about 8 minutes. Transfer to a bowl and refrigerate for at least 30 minutes.

2. In a large mixing bowl, combine the butter and salt until smooth. Add the cooled mixture from the refrigerator and the egg and continue to beat until frosting-like.

3. Once fully mixed, add the flour, baking soda, and baking powder. Continue mixing until combined, then add green food coloring to get a medium green color like in the movie. Fold in the caramel chips.

4. Using your hands, roll the dough into 2-inch balls and place on a parchment-lined baking sheet (should make approximately 24 dough balls). Chill in the freezer for at least an hour.

5. Preheat the oven to 350°F. Transfer the balls to 2 parchment-lined baking sheets. Space the balls at least 4 inches apart.

6. Bake until the edges start to brown, about 15 minutes. Cool and serve!

THE LAZY MARY

12 ounces frozen strawberries
12 ounces frozen raspberries
12 ounces frozen cherries
1 (750-ml) bottle sauvignon blanc

KILL LEVEL: Easy | BODY COUNT: 1 batch | PREP TIME: 5 minutes

TIP: When you're blending the slushie, make sure the lid to the blender or food processor is on extra tight. I had a bit of an explosion the first time I made this, and I was cleaning berries off the ceiling for days.

1. Add the frozen berries and the bottle of wine to a blender or food processor. Make sure everything is tightly shut. Blend until only slightly chunky. If everything doesn't fit in the blender at once, you can blend in batches. If you're making batches, simply combine all batches together when done.

2. Serve in a chilled wine glass!

DRINKING GAME
Take a drink every time someone uses the wrong key in a door.

THE CONJURING (2013)

Even on the chilling poster itself, a noose can be seen prominently hanging from a creepy old tree, which just so happens to be a central plot point in the film.

ROPE NOOSES

Braided Puff Pastries Two Ways: Chocolate Raspberry and Chocolate Marshmallow

2 sheets frozen puff pastry

3 tablespoons raspberry jam

3 tablespoons marshmallow fluff

10 ounces milk chocolate chips

1 large egg

¼ page cup powdered sugar

KILL LEVEL: Moderate | BODY COUNT: 6 servings | PREP TIME: 15 minutes | COOK TIME: 20 minutes

TIP: You can fill the rope nooses with any flavors you like. Try Nutella and peanut butter or strawberry and banana. The possibilities are endless. Just be creative.

1. Preheat the oven to 425°F. Allow both sheets of frozen pastry to thaw. Once thawed, lay each one on separate baking sheets lined with parchment paper. The dough should unfold into 3 sections.

2. Make 7 slightly sloped cuts down both the left and right sections of the dough, about 2 inches apart. The cuts should stop about an inch from the center section. The two sides should be mirror images.

3. In the center section of one of the pastries, spread the raspberry jam. In the center of the other, spread the marshmallow fluff.

4. Sprinkle an even amount of chocolate chips on both sections of spread.

5. To braid, fold the top and bottom of each pastry about an inch over the chocolate first, then cross the side strips tightly over one another.

6. Meanwhile, beat the egg with a splash of water and brush the egg wash on top of each braided pastry.

7. Bake for approximately 20 minutes, or until the tops are golden brown. Remove from the oven, let cool, and then sprinkle with powdered sugar. Slice and serve!

THE HIDE AND CLAP

3 ounces vodka

3 ounces Kahlúa

½ cup coconut milk from a carton

KILL LEVEL: Easy | **BODY COUNT:** 1 drink | **PREP TIME:** 5 minutes

1. Put everything into a shaker with ice. Shake well and pour the contents into a rocks glass. Serve!

DRINKING GAME

Take a drink every time a door opens, closes, or is knocked on.

JAWS (1975)

Who can forget the "get out of the water" scene where that kid is just minding his business on his floatie while the shark approaches from beneath? Poor Alex.

BLOODY FLOATIES
Fried Donuts with Homemade Red Velvet Ice Cream

FOR THE RED VELVET ICE CREAM:

8 ounces cream cheese, room temperature

2 cups heavy cream

¾ cup granulated sugar

2 tablespoons red food coloring

2 tablespoons cocoa powder

½ teaspoon salt

FOR THE FRIED DONUTS:

1 can Pillsbury Grands Biscuits

vegetable oil, for frying

KILL LEVEL: Moderate | **BODY COUNT:** 6 servings | **PREP TIME:** 15 minutes | **COOK TIME:** 35 minutes

1. Start with the ice cream. Place all the ingredients in a blender and pulse until smooth.

2. Pour the mixture into an ice cream maker and follow the manufacturer's directions. Once finished, place in the freezer overnight.

3. Once the ice cream is set, open the can of biscuits and place the biscuits on a baking sheet. Use a small round cookie cutter or shot glass rim to cut a hole in the middle of each biscuit.

4. Pour oil into a skillet to the depth of about ½ inch. Heat the oil over medium to medium-high heat for about 5 minutes. To test if your oil is hot enough, lightly place one of your donut holes into the oil. If it sizzles and starts to brown, it is ready.

5. Once the oil is hot, fry each biscuit—one or two at a time to avoid crowding—until golden on both sides. You'll have to keep an eye on them to know when they are done, but it usually takes approximately 1 to 2 minutes per side.

6. Remove each batch of finished donuts (and donut holes, of course) from the oil and place on a paper towel–lined plate.

7. Place each donut on its own plate and top with a scoop of the ice cream. Watch as it begins to melt and looks like blood dripping over the donut floatie.

TIPS: If you don't have an ice cream maker, I highly recommend buying one. Nothing beats homemade ice cream. In the meantime, I suggest searching online for how to make ice cream without an ice cream maker. Also, if you would rather leave the biscuits whole and pipe them full of jam or custard, that would also be delicious. It just won't look as much like a floatie.

THE SHARK BITE

1 ounce vodka

1 ounce triple sec

2 ounces blue Curaçao

3 maraschino cherries, muddled

2 tablespoons cherry juice from jar

KILL LEVEL: Easy | BODY COUNT: 1 drink | PREP TIME: 5 minutes

1. Shake all vodka, triple sec, and blue Curaçao together in a shaker over ice.

2. Pour into a rocks glass over ice, and top with the muddled cherries. Slowly drizzle the cherry juice over the cherries so it looks like blood seeping into the water.

DRINKING GAME

Take a drink every time you hear the iconic theme music.

BUG (2006)

This intense examination of paranoia is from the same man who directed *The Exorcist*. In this film, our leads isolate themselves from the outside world, sealing themselves in their room and covering it with flypaper and aluminum foil and lighting it with the glow from bug zappers.

FLYPAPER
Honey-Glazed Lemon Bars Topped with Chocolate Chip "Bugs"

FOR THE CRUST:

1 cup butter, melted

½ cup granulated sugar

1 tablespoon vanilla extract

¼ teaspoon salt

2 cups all-purpose flour

FOR THE FILLING:

2 cups granulated sugar

5 tablespoons all-purpose flour

6 large eggs

1 cup fresh lemon juice (4 to 6 lemons)

¼ cup honey

1 cup chocolate chips

KILL LEVEL: Easy | BODY COUNT: 8 to 10 servings | PREP TIME: 10 minutes plus an hour to chill | COOK TIME: 45 minutes

1. Preheat the oven to 325°F. Line the bottom of a 9 x 13-inch baking pan with parchment paper. Leave some paper hanging over the sides for easy lifting.

2. To make the crust, mix the melted butter, sugar, vanilla, and salt together in a large bowl. Add the flour and stir to combine. The dough will be thick. Press it firmly into the bottom of the baking pan, making sure it is even.

3. Bake for 20 minutes, or until the edges are lightly browned. While the crust is still warm, gently poke a few shallow holes throughout with a fork, but don't pierce all the way through the dough. Set aside.

4. To make the filling, mix the sugar and flour together in a large bowl. Add the eggs and lemon juice and whisk until smooth.

5. Pour the filling over the crust and bake for another 25 minutes, or until the filling has set and no longer jiggles. Remove from the oven. While the filling is still warm, pour the honey on top and spread it all over. Let cool.

6. Once the filling is at room temperature, sprinkle the chocolate chips evenly over the honey. The filling should be just warm enough for them to stick but not melt.

7. Place the pan in the refrigerator for at least an hour. Once chilled, remove from fridge and cut into squares. Serve cold.

THE HEMOLYMPH

2 ounces green crème de menthe
2 ounces clear chocolate liqueur
½ cup almond milk

KILL LEVEL: Easy | **BODY COUNT:** 1 drink | **PREP TIME:** 5 minutes

TIP: If you can find only clear crème de menthe, you can always add a few drops of green food coloring to the shaker.

1. Add all the ingredients to a shaker with ice.

2. Shake well and pour the contents into a rocks glass.

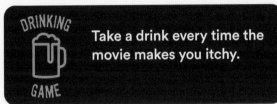

DRINKING GAME

Take a drink every time the movie makes you itchy.

NIGHT OF THE LIVING DEAD (1968)

Dead bodies are straight up digging their way out of their graves in this classic first feature from horror master George Romero.

BURIAL PLOT
Pudding, Whipped Cream, and Crushed Oreo Dirt Dessert

8 ounces cream cheese, softened

½ cup butter, softened

¾ cup powdered sugar

2 small boxes instant vanilla pudding

3 cups whole milk, cold

1 (12-ounce) tub whipped topping, like Cool Whip

1 pound Oreos, crushed

creepy crawly candies (optional)

KILL LEVEL: Easy | **BODY COUNT:** 6 servings | **PREP TIME:** 20 minutes

1. Using a mixer, combine the cream cheese, butter, and powdered sugar.

2. In a separate large bowl, using a mixer, combine the pudding and milk until thickened.

3. Fold the whipped topping into the pudding, then fold in the cream cheese mixture until smooth.

4. In a large bowl or casserole dish, alternate layers of pudding mixture with crushed Oreos. Scoop onto individual plates or bowls and top with your favorite creepy crawly candies, if using.

TIP: If you want to be classy, you can serve the dessert in individual *plots*. Just follow the layering instructions, but use individual martini glasses.

THE FARMHOUSE

1 ounce mezcal
1 ounce apple brandy
2 ounces amaretto liqueur
2 tablespoons pure maple syrup
1 dash of angostura bitters

1. Add all the ingredients to a shaker over ice and shake well.

2. Pour the contents into a rocks glass over ice and serve!

KILL LEVEL: Easy | BODY COUNT: 1 drink | PREP TIME: 5 minutes

DRINKING GAME

Take a drink every time Harry is a douchebag. Pace yourself.

BLACK CHRISTMAS (1974)

What's Christmas without Christmas carols?

I'M DREAMING OF A BLACK CHRISTMAS

Jet-Black Panna Cotta with a Surprise Holiday Flavor

½ ounce unflavored gelatin

6 tablespoons water, cold

6 cups heavy cream

1 cup granulated sugar

6 ounces white chocolate, chopped

2 teaspoons pure peppermint extract

10 (or more) drops of black food coloring

KILL LEVEL: Moderate | BODY COUNT: 6 servings | PREP TIME: 10 minutes plus 2 hours to refrigerate | COOK TIME: 5 minutes

TIP: The dessert is supposed to be like ripping open a Christmas present, a surprise flavor reveal as you take your first bite. Because it is black, you can hide any flavor in there. If you don't like peppermint, try other holiday extracts like rum or gingerbread or apple cinnamon. The possibilities are endless and the surprise is always fun.

1. In a small bowl, sprinkle gelatin over the cold water. Let sit for 10 minutes.

2. In a medium saucepan over medium heat, bring the cream and sugar to a simmer. Add the gelatin mixture and stir for 2 minutes, or until the gelatin and sugar are dissolved.

3. In a large glass bowl, melt the white chocolate in the microwave in 30-second increments. Be careful not to burn the chocolate.

4. Transfer the mixture from the saucepan to the large glass bowl with the melted chocolate and whisk until cool, about 7 minutes. Stir in the peppermint extract and food coloring, then divide the mixture among 6 ramekins. Refrigerate for at least 2 hours.

5. Once the mixture is set, remove the ramekins from the fridge and place them in a roasting pan filled with 1 inch of hot water. Make sure you don't fill the pan too high with water. You don't want it to get in the ramekins. The sides of the panna cotta should begin to melt slightly, loosening them up enough to flip them onto a plate and out of the ramekins. The best way to get them out is by placing the face of the plate on top of the ramekin and flipping both together.

THE OPEN FIRE

FOR THE CHESTNUT MILK (BATCH):
1 cup roasted chestnuts
1 quart almond milk

FOR THE OPEN FIRE:
½ cup Chestnut Milk
1 ounce amaretto
3 ounces white chocolate liqueur
dash of allspice (optional)

KILL LEVEL: Moderate | **BODY COUNT:** 1 drink |
PREP TIME: 10 minutes

1. To make the chestnut milk, put the chestnuts and the almond milk into a blender. Blend until smooth, then drain through a cheesecloth into a container with a lid. Refrigerate until needed.

2. For the drink, pour the liquid ingredients into a rocks glass over ice and give a quick stir. Garnish with a dash of allspice if you like.

DRINKING GAME

Take a drink every time someone says "Christmas."

CABIN FEVER (2002)

There is nothing—I mean NOTHING—more disgusting than Marcy taking a bath.
(I should also mention that my guests still have wet dreams about this dessert.)

THE CLOSE SHAVE
Pavlova with Crème Chantilly and Berry Compote

FOR THE PAVLOVA:

5 egg whites

1¼ cups granulated sugar

2 teaspoons cornstarch

1 teaspoon white vinegar

¼ teaspoon salt

2 tablespoons vanilla extract

FOR THE BERRY COMPOTE:

2 cups frozen mixed berries

1 tablespoon granulated sugar

FOR THE CRÈME CHANTILLY:

1½ cups heavy cream

2 tablespoons granulated sugar

2 teaspoons vanilla extract

pinch of salt

KILL LEVEL: Hard | BODY COUNT: 8 servings |
PREP TIME: 10 minutes plus 1 hour to chill |
COOK TIME: 1 hour

1. Line a baking sheet with parchment paper and preheat the oven to 250°F.

2. To make the pavlova, beat the egg whites on high speed in a mixing bowl until soft peaks begin to form. Very slowly sprinkle the sugar into the egg whites, then reduce speed to low and continue to mix. Add the cornstarch, vinegar, salt, and vanilla extract. Continue to beat on high until the mixture becomes glossy and stiff peaks form.

3. Scoop the pavlova onto the baking sheet and form it into a circle with the sides noticeably higher than the middle. Bake until the edges are crispy and only very slightly beige, about 1 hour. Turn the oven off, open the door, and allow the meringue to cool in the oven.

4. Meanwhile, in a medium saucepan, add the berries and sugar and cook over medium heat until the mixture begins to blend, about 20 minutes. Set aside to cool.

5. Once the berries are cool, refrigerate them for at least an hour. The compote will thicken a bit for gore factor, but runny is just as good.

6. Whip all the ingredients for the crème chantilly until firm peaks form.

7. Move the cooled and hardened pavlova to a serving platter, top it with the crème chantilly, then pour the cold berry compote on top. Does it look like Marcy's leg after she shaved? It should.

> **TIP:** You must follow the pavlova instructions exactly or it will not turn out correctly and you will have to start over. Don't rush the process and try to combine everything all at once. A pavlova takes patience but is worth it.

PANCAKES!!!!

1 strip cooked bacon, for garnish
2 ounces Irish whiskey
2 ounces butterscotch schnapps
¼ cup orange juice
2 tablespoons pure maple syrup

KILL LEVEL: Easy | **BODY COUNT:** 1 drink |
PREP TIME: 5 minutes | **COOK TIME:** 20 minutes

1. Preheat the oven to 400° F. Bake 1 strip of bacon (or as much as you can handle) on a foil-lined baking sheet for 20 minutes.

2. For the drink, pour all the liquid ingredients into a shaker with ice. Shake it well.

3. Dump the contents into a pint glass and garnish with the bacon strip.

DRINKING GAME

Take a drink every time the deputy says "party."

TUCKER AND DALE VS. EVIL (2010)

Oh, man. Such a funny movie. Remember when Tucker sawed into a bee's nest?

BEE STING CAKE

Vanilla Cake Stuffed with Honey Cream and Topped with Candied Almonds

FOR THE CAKE:

2 large eggs
¾ cup Splenda flakes
1 cup all-purpose flour
1 teaspoon baking powder
pinch of salt
½ cup almond milk
1 tablespoon butter
1 tablespoon honey

FOR THE TOPPING:

¼ cup butter
¼ cup Splenda flakes
1½ tablespoons honey
1 tablespoon heavy cream
1 cup slivered almonds
1 teaspoon vanilla extract

FOR THE HONEY CREAM:

2 cups whipping cream
2 tablespoons Splenda flakes
2 tablespoons honey
3 heaping tablespoons instant vanilla pudding powder

KILL LEVEL: Hard | **BODY COUNT:** 6 servings | **PREP TIME:** 15 minutes | **COOK TIME:** 40 minutes

TIP: If you're serious about entertaining, you really should have a 6-inch springform pan in your arsenal.

1. Preheat the oven to 350°F.

2. To make the cake, in a large bowl, mix the eggs and Splenda until thick and creamy. Add the flour, baking powder, and salt, and continue to mix until combined.

3. In a saucepan, heat the milk, butter, and honey over medium heat to just about boiling, about 5 minutes. Give it a stir and mix it into the batter.

4. Pour the mixture into a greased 6-inch springform pan. Bake for about 25 minutes, until firm to touch and a wooden toothpick inserted into the center comes out clean.

5. Meanwhile, make the topping. In a small pan over low heat, melt the butter. Add the Splenda, honey, and heavy cream, stirring continually.

6. Bring to a gentle boil for about 5 minutes, then stir in the almonds and vanilla. Set aside to cool slightly. Carefully spread the topping on the cake evenly and immediately as it comes out of the oven.

7. Set the oven to broil and broil the cake for a few minutes, until the top is browned. Keep an eye on it. Be careful not to burn it!

8. Let the cake cool. Once cool, remove it carefully from the springform pan. If it is sticking, gently use a knife to separate the topping from the sides.

9. To make the honey cream, whip the cream, Splenda, honey, and vanilla pudding powder until very stiff, almost a whipped butter consistency but not quite. I find that for this recipe, the thicker the cream the better. Just be careful not to overdo it or it will turn into butter and you will have to add more cream to fix it.

10. Once the cake is completely cool, cut it in half horizontally. Spread the honey cream on the bottom half. Cut the top half into 6 equal wedges and place them carefully on top of the honey cream. This will help you cut the cake later.

11. Keep refrigerated until ready to serve or the honey cream might fall and the cake will collapse.

TIP: If you would rather not use Splenda flakes, you can substitute granulated sugar in equal parts.

THE WOOD CHIPPER

1 ounce Ole Smokey Tennessee Moonshine
1 ounce strawberry jam
½ cup strawberry soda

KILL LEVEL: Easy | **BODY COUNT:** 1 drink | **PREP TIME:** 5 minutes

1. Add the moonshine and jam to a blender, and blend until combined.

2. Pour the mixture into a rocks glass over ice, add the soda, and give a stir. Serve extra cold!

DRINKING GAME

Take a drink every time someone says "hillbilly" or "college kid."

CONVERSIONS

VOLUME

US	US Equivalent	Metric
1 tablespoon (3 teaspoons)	½ fluid ounce	15 milliliters
¼ cup	2 fluid ounces	60 milliliters
⅓ cup	3 fluid ounces	90 milliliters
½ cup	4 fluid ounces	120 milliliters
⅔ cup	5 fluid ounces	150 milliliters
¾ cup	6 fluid ounces	180 milliliters
1 cup	8 fluid ounces	240 milliliters
2 cups	16 fluid ounces	480 milliliters

WEIGHT

US	Metric
½ ounce	15 grams
1 ounce	30 grams
2 ounces	60 grams
¼ pound	115 grams
⅓ pound	150 grams
½ pound	225 grams
¾ pound	350 grams
1 pound	450 grams

TEMPERATURE

Fahrenheit (°F)	Celsius (°C)	Fahrenheit (°F)	Celsius (°C)
70°F	20°C	220°F	105°C
100°F	40°C	240°F	115°C
120°F	50°C	260°F	125°C
130°F	55°C	280°F	140°C
140°F	60°C	300°F	150°C
150°F	65°C	325°F	165°C
160°F	70°C	350°F	175°C
170°F	75°C	375°F	190°C
180°F	80°C	400°F	200°C
190°F	90°C	425°F	220°C
200°F	95°C	450°F	230°C

ACKNOWLEDGMENTS

No humans were harmed in the creation of this cookbook, but I would like to thank all the lovely lab rats who volunteered to let me experiment on them with these bloody good recipes. I couldn't have done any of this without you.

I'd also like to thank Josh, my slicing and dicing partner. Your constant love and encouragement make it so easy for me to try new things, be creative, and take risks. I love you.

ABOUT THE AUTHOR

Richard S. Sargent was born and raised in Pittsburgh, Pennsylvania. Some of his earliest memories are of sitting in front of the TV after school, watching reruns of *Chiller Theatre* with his mom. You can blame her for his obsession with horror films.

Richard is an award-winning actor, director, producer, playwright, and filmmaker. You can find some of his short plays published on Amazon via Left Coast Publishing. His short film, *Meat*, described as "torture porn with bacon," was released in the horror anthology World of Death.

Richard has always been interested in creative cooking. Most of his day jobs were in restaurants and on food trucks. After taking a few cooking classes, Richard decided doing it for a living would take all of the fun out of it. So he found a new way to keep cooking fun: *The Horror Movie Night Cookbook*!

When he isn't doing theater, cooking for his friends, or watching horror films, he is performing with the band he and his husband created—The Green Winter. You can listen to their music on iTunes and Spotify. Follow Richard on Facebook and Instagram to see what's coming next.

NOTES